My Psychic Journal

MELISSA ALVAREZ

Adrema Press

Author Websites: www.MelissaAlvarez.com and www.APsychicHaven.com

ISBN: 978-1-59611-113-4

Cover and Book Design by Melissa Alvarez at BookCovers.Us

First Trade Paperback Printing: June 2013
10 9 8 7 6 5 4 3 2 1

Other books by Melissa Alvarez

365 Ways to Raise Your Frequency
The 365 Days to Raise Your Frequency Journal
Your Psychic Self
Simply Give Thanks
Simply Give Thanks Gratitude Journal
Analyze Your Handwriting
Your Color Power
Ghosts, A Spirit Guide and A Past Life
Chakra Divination® Cards & Charts Activity Book
The Essential Guide To Chakra Divination
Chakra Divination Ultimate Balance Journal
The eLink Directory of Paranormal Investigative Groups Around the World
Homemade Recipes for Horse Treats plus Fly Sprays & Tips for Owners
The Phoenix's Guide To Self Renewal
Christmas Desserts
Penelope Panda's Shooting Star

Writing as Ariana Dupré
Paranormal Romantic Suspense

Night Visions
Paradise Designs
Briar Mountain
Talgorian Dragon
Talgorian Prophecy

Websites:
MelissaA.com
BookCoversGalore.com
BookCovers.Us
APsychicHaven.com

Date: ________________

Today's Intuitions and Psychic Events:

Date: ________________

Today's Intuitions and Psychic Events: ________________________

Date: ________________

*Today's Intuitions and Psychic Events:*________________________

Date: ________________

*Today's Intuitions and Psychic Events:*________________________

Date: ________________

*Today's Intuitions and Psychic Events:*________________________

Date: ________________

Today's Intuitions and Psychic Events: ________________________

Date: ________________

Today's Intuitions and Psychic Events: ______________________

Date: ________________

*Today's Intuitions and Psychic Events:*________________________

Date: ______________

Today's Intuitions and Psychic Events: ______________

Date: ________________

*Today's Intuitions and Psychic Events:*________________________

Date: ________________

Today's Intuitions and Psychic Events:

Date: ________________

Today's Intuitions and Psychic Events: ________________________

Date: ________________

Today's Intuitions and Psychic Events:

Date: ________________

*Today's Intuitions and Psychic Events:*________________________

Date: ________________

Today's Intuitions and Psychic Events: ________________________

Date: ________________

*Today's Intuitions and Psychic Events:*________________________

Date: ______________

*Today's Intuitions and Psychic Events:*______________________

Date: ________________

Today's Intuitions and Psychic Events: ________________________

Date: ________________

*Today's Intuitions and Psychic Events:*________________________

Date: ________________

Today's Intuitions and Psychic Events: ________________

Date: ________________

Today's Intuitions and Psychic Events:

Date: ________________

*Today's Intuitions and Psychic Events:*________________________

Date: ________________

Today's Intuitions and Psychic Events: ________________________

Date: ______________

Today's Intuitions and Psychic Events: ____________________

Date: ________________

*Today's Intuitions and Psychic Events:*________________________

Date: ________________

Today's Intuitions and Psychic Events: ________________________

Date: ________________

*Today's Intuitions and Psychic Events:*________________________

Date: ________________

*Today's Intuitions and Psychic Events:*________________________

Date: ________________

*Today's Intuitions and Psychic Events:*________________________

Date: ________________

*Today's Intuitions and Psychic Events:*________________________

Date: ________________

*Today's Intuitions and Psychic Events:*________________________

Date: ________________

Today's Intuitions and Psychic Events: ________________________

Date: ________________

Today's Intuitions and Psychic Events:

Date: ________________

*Today's Intuitions and Psychic Events:*________________________

Date: ________________

*Today's Intuitions and Psychic Events:*________________________

Date: ______________

*Today's Intuitions and Psychic Events:*______________________

Date: ________________

*Today's Intuitions and Psychic Events:*________________________

Date: ________________

Today's Intuitions and Psychic Events: ________________________

Date: ______________

*Today's Intuitions and Psychic Events:*______________________

Date: ________________

*Today's Intuitions and Psychic Events:*________________________

Date: __________________

*Today's Intuitions and Psychic Events:*__________________________

Date: ________________

*Today's Intuitions and Psychic Events:*________________________

Date: ________________

Today's Intuitions and Psychic Events: ________________________

Date: _______________

Today's Intuitions and Psychic Events: ________________________

Date: ________________

Today's Intuitions and Psychic Events:

Date: ________________

*Today's Intuitions and Psychic Events:*________________________

Date: ________________

*Today's Intuitions and Psychic Events:*________________________

Date: ________________

*Today's Intuitions and Psychic Events:*________________________

Date: ________________

*Today's Intuitions and Psychic Events:*________________________

Date: ________________

Today's Intuitions and Psychic Events: ________________________

Date: ________________

Today's Intuitions and Psychic Events:

Date: ________________

*Today's Intuitions and Psychic Events:*________________________

Date: ________________

Today's Intuitions and Psychic Events:________________________

Date: ________________

*Today's Intuitions and Psychic Events:*______________________

Date: ________________

*Today's Intuitions and Psychic Events:*________________________

Date: ________________

Today's Intuitions and Psychic Events:

Date: ________________

Today's Intuitions and Psychic Events:

Date: ________________

*Today's Intuitions and Psychic Events:*________________________

Date: ________________

*Today's Intuitions and Psychic Events:*________________________

Date: ______________

Today's Intuitions and Psychic Events: ______________________

Date: ________________

*Today's Intuitions and Psychic Events:*________________________

Date: ________________

Today's Intuitions and Psychic Events: ________________________

Date: ______________

Today's Intuitions and Psychic Events: ______________________

Date: ________________

Today's Intuitions and Psychic Events: ________________________

Date: ________________

*Today's Intuitions and Psychic Events:*________________________

Date: ________________

Today's Intuitions and Psychic Events:________________________

Date: ________________

*Today's Intuitions and Psychic Events:*________________________

Date: ________________

Today's Intuitions and Psychic Events: ____________________

Date: ________________

Today's Intuitions and Psychic Events: ________________________

Date: ________________

*Today's Intuitions and Psychic Events:*________________________

Date: ________________

Today's Intuitions and Psychic Events:________________________

Date: ________________

Today's Intuitions and Psychic Events: ________________________

Date: ________________

Today's Intuitions and Psychic Events:

Date: ________________

Today's Intuitions and Psychic Events: ________________________

Date: ________________

*Today's Intuitions and Psychic Events:*________________________

Date: ________________

Today's Intuitions and Psychic Events: ________________________

Date: ______________

Today's Intuitions and Psychic Events:

Date: ________________

*Today's Intuitions and Psychic Events:*________________________

Date: ______________

*Today's Intuitions and Psychic Events:*______________________

Date: _______________

Today's Intuitions and Psychic Events: ________________________

Date: ________________

*Today's Intuitions and Psychic Events:*________________________

Date: ________________

*Today's Intuitions and Psychic Events:*________________________

Date: ________________

*Today's Intuitions and Psychic Events:*________________________

Date: ________________

Today's Intuitions and Psychic Events: ________________________

Date: ________________

Today's Intuitions and Psychic Events:

Date: ________________

Today's Intuitions and Psychic Events: ________________________

Date: ________________

*Today's Intuitions and Psychic Events:*________________________

Date: ________________

*Today's Intuitions and Psychic Events:*________________________

Date: ________________

Today's Intuitions and Psychic Events:

Date: ________________

*Today's Intuitions and Psychic Events:*________________________

Date: ________________

*Today's Intuitions and Psychic Events:*________________________

Date: ________________

*Today's Intuitions and Psychic Events:*________________________

Date: ________________

*Today's Intuitions and Psychic Events:*________________________

Date: ________________

*Today's Intuitions and Psychic Events:*________________________

Date: ________________

*Today's Intuitions and Psychic Events:*________________________

Date: ________________

Today's Intuitions and Psychic Events: ________________________

Date: ________________

Today's Intuitions and Psychic Events: ________________________

Date: ________________

Today's Intuitions and Psychic Events: ________________________

Date: ________________

*Today's Intuitions and Psychic Events:*________________________

Date: ________________

Today's Intuitions and Psychic Events: ________________________

Date: ______________

*Today's Intuitions and Psychic Events:*______________________

Date: ________________

*Today's Intuitions and Psychic Events:*________________________

Date: ______________

*Today's Intuitions and Psychic Events:*______________________

Date: ________________

Today's Intuitions and Psychic Events: ________________________

Date: ________________

Today's Intuitions and Psychic Events:

Date: ________________

*Today's Intuitions and Psychic Events:*________________________

Date: ________________

Today's Intuitions and Psychic Events: ________________________

Date: ________________

*Today's Intuitions and Psychic Events:*________________________

Date: ________________

*Today's Intuitions and Psychic Events:*________________________

Date: ________________

Today's Intuitions and Psychic Events: ________________________

Date: ________________

Today's Intuitions and Psychic Events:

Date: ________________

Today's Intuitions and Psychic Events: ________________________

Date: ________________

*Today's Intuitions and Psychic Events:*________________________

Date: ________________

*Today's Intuitions and Psychic Events:*________________________

Date: _______________

*Today's Intuitions and Psychic Events:*______________________

Date: ________________

Today's Intuitions and Psychic Events: ________________________

Date: ________________

*Today's Intuitions and Psychic Events:*________________________

Date: ________________

Today's Intuitions and Psychic Events: ________________________

Date: ________________

Today's Intuitions and Psychic Events: ________________________

Date: ______________

*Today's Intuitions and Psychic Events:*______________________

Date: ________________

Today's Intuitions and Psychic Events:

Date: ________________

Today's Intuitions and Psychic Events:________________________

Date: ________________

*Today's Intuitions and Psychic Events:*________________________

Date: ________________

*Today's Intuitions and Psychic Events:*________________________

Date: ________________

Today's Intuitions and Psychic Events:

Date: ________________

*Today's Intuitions and Psychic Events:*________________________

Date: ________________

*Today's Intuitions and Psychic Events:*________________________

Date: ________________

Today's Intuitions and Psychic Events: ________________________

Date: ________________

Today's Intuitions and Psychic Events:

Date: ________________

*Today's Intuitions and Psychic Events:*________________________

Date: ______________

*Today's Intuitions and Psychic Events:*______________________

Date: ________________

*Today's Intuitions and Psychic Events:*________________________

Date: ________________

Today's Intuitions and Psychic Events:

Date: ________________

Today's Intuitions and Psychic Events: ________________________

Date: ________________

*Today's Intuitions and Psychic Events:*________________________

Date: ________________

*Today's Intuitions and Psychic Events:*________________________

Date: ________________

Today's Intuitions and Psychic Events:

Date: ________________

Today's Intuitions and Psychic Events: ________________________

Date: ________________

*Today's Intuitions and Psychic Events:*________________________

Date: ________________

Today's Intuitions and Psychic Events: ________________________

Date: ________________

*Today's Intuitions and Psychic Events:*________________________

Date: ________________

*Today's Intuitions and Psychic Events:*________________________

Date: ________________

*Today's Intuitions and Psychic Events:*________________________

Date: ________________

Today's Intuitions and Psychic Events: ________________________

Date: ________________

*Today's Intuitions and Psychic Events:*________________________

Date: ________________

Today's Intuitions and Psychic Events:

Date: ________________

Today's Intuitions and Psychic Events:

Date: ________________

*Today's Intuitions and Psychic Events:*________________________

Date: ________________

*Today's Intuitions and Psychic Events:*________________________

Date: ________________

Today's Intuitions and Psychic Events: ______________________

Date: ________________

*Today's Intuitions and Psychic Events:*______________________

Date: ________________

Today's Intuitions and Psychic Events: ________________________

Date: ________________

*Today's Intuitions and Psychic Events:*________________________

Date: ________________

Today's Intuitions and Psychic Events:

Date: ________________

*Today's Intuitions and Psychic Events:*________________________

Date: ________________

*Today's Intuitions and Psychic Events:*________________________

Date: ________________

*Today's Intuitions and Psychic Events:*________________________

Date: ________________

Today's Intuitions and Psychic Events: ________________________

Date: ________________

*Today's Intuitions and Psychic Events:*________________________

Date: ________________

*Today's Intuitions and Psychic Events:*________________________

Date: ________________

*Today's Intuitions and Psychic Events:*________________________

Date: ________________

Today's Intuitions and Psychic Events: ________________________

Date: ________________

*Today's Intuitions and Psychic Events:*________________________

Date: ________________

*Today's Intuitions and Psychic Events:*________________________

Date: ______________

*Today's Intuitions and Psychic Events:*______________________

Date: ________________

*Today's Intuitions and Psychic Events:*________________________

Date: ________________

*Today's Intuitions and Psychic Events:*________________________

Date: ________________

*Today's Intuitions and Psychic Events:*_______________________

Date: ________________

*Today's Intuitions and Psychic Events:*______________________

Date: ________________

Today's Intuitions and Psychic Events: ________________________

Date: ________________

*Today's Intuitions and Psychic Events:*________________________

Date: ________________

*Today's Intuitions and Psychic Events:*________________________

Date: ________________

*Today's Intuitions and Psychic Events:*________________________

Date: ________________

Today's Intuitions and Psychic Events: ________________________

Date: ________________

Today's Intuitions and Psychic Events:

Date: ________________

*Today's Intuitions and Psychic Events:*________________________

Date: ________________

*Today's Intuitions and Psychic Events:*________________________

Date: ________________

*Today's Intuitions and Psychic Events:*________________________

Date: ________________

*Today's Intuitions and Psychic Events:*________________________

Date: ________________

Today's Intuitions and Psychic Events: ________________________

Date: ______________

*Today's Intuitions and Psychic Events:*______________________

Date: ________________

Today's Intuitions and Psychic Events: ________________________

Date: _______________

*Today's Intuitions and Psychic Events:*______________________

Date: ________________

*Today's Intuitions and Psychic Events:*________________________

Date: _______________

Today's Intuitions and Psychic Events:

Date: ________________

*Today's Intuitions and Psychic Events:*________________________

Date: ________________

*Today's Intuitions and Psychic Events:*________________________

Date: ________________

Today's Intuitions and Psychic Events: ________________________

Date: ________________

*Today's Intuitions and Psychic Events:*________________________

Date: ________________

Today's Intuitions and Psychic Events:

Date: ________________

Today's Intuitions and Psychic Events:

Date: ________________

*Today's Intuitions and Psychic Events:*________________________

Date: ________________

Today's Intuitions and Psychic Events:

Date: ________________

Today's Intuitions and Psychic Events: ________________________

Date: ________________

*Today's Intuitions and Psychic Events:*________________________

Date: ________________

*Today's Intuitions and Psychic Events:*________________________

Date: ________________

*Today's Intuitions and Psychic Events:*________________________

Date: ________________

*Today's Intuitions and Psychic Events:*________________________

Date: ________________

*Today's Intuitions and Psychic Events:*________________________

Date: ________________

Today's Intuitions and Psychic Events: ________________________

Date: ________________

Today's Intuitions and Psychic Events:

Date: ________________

Today's Intuitions and Psychic Events: ________________________

Date: ________________

*Today's Intuitions and Psychic Events:*________________________

Date: ________________

*Today's Intuitions and Psychic Events:*________________________

Date: ________________

*Today's Intuitions and Psychic Events:*________________________

Date: ________________

Today's Intuitions and Psychic Events: ________________________

Date: ________________

*Today's Intuitions and Psychic Events:*________________________

Date: ________________

Today's Intuitions and Psychic Events: ________________________

Date: ________________

*Today's Intuitions and Psychic Events:*________________________

Date: ________________

*Today's Intuitions and Psychic Events:*________________________

Date: ______________

*Today's Intuitions and Psychic Events:*______________________

Date: ________________

*Today's Intuitions and Psychic Events:*________________________

Date: ________________

*Today's Intuitions and Psychic Events:*________________________

Date: ________________

Today's Intuitions and Psychic Events: ________________________

Date: ______________

*Today's Intuitions and Psychic Events:*______________________

Date: ________________

*Today's Intuitions and Psychic Events:*________________________

Date: ________________

*Today's Intuitions and Psychic Events:*________________________

Date: ________________

Today's Intuitions and Psychic Events:

Date: ________________

Today's Intuitions and Psychic Events:

Date: ________________

*Today's Intuitions and Psychic Events:*________________________

Date: ________________

*Today's Intuitions and Psychic Events:*________________________

Date: ________________

Today's Intuitions and Psychic Events: ________________________

Date: ________________

Today's Intuitions and Psychic Events: ________________________

Date: ________________

Today's Intuitions and Psychic Events: ________________________

Date: ________________

Today's Intuitions and Psychic Events: ________________________

Date: ________________

Today's Intuitions and Psychic Events:

Date: ________________

Today's Intuitions and Psychic Events: ________________________

Date: ________________

Today's Intuitions and Psychic Events: ________________________

Date: ________________

*Today's Intuitions and Psychic Events:*________________________

Date: ________________

*Today's Intuitions and Psychic Events:*________________________

Date: ________________

*Today's Intuitions and Psychic Events:*________________________

Date: ________________

Today's Intuitions and Psychic Events: ________________________

Date: ______________

*Today's Intuitions and Psychic Events:*______________________

Date: ________________

*Today's Intuitions and Psychic Events:*________________________

Date: ________________

*Today's Intuitions and Psychic Events:*________________________

Date: ________________

Today's Intuitions and Psychic Events: ________________________

Date: ______________

*Today's Intuitions and Psychic Events:*______________________

Date: ________________

*Today's Intuitions and Psychic Events:*________________________

Date: ______________

Today's Intuitions and Psychic Events:

Date: ________________

*Today's Intuitions and Psychic Events:*________________________

Date: ________________

*Today's Intuitions and Psychic Events:*________________________

Date: ________________

*Today's Intuitions and Psychic Events:*________________________

Date: ________________

*Today's Intuitions and Psychic Events:*________________________

Date: ______________

Today's Intuitions and Psychic Events: ______________________

Date: ________________

*Today's Intuitions and Psychic Events:*________________________

Date: ________________

*Today's Intuitions and Psychic Events:*________________________

Date: ________________

*Today's Intuitions and Psychic Events:*________________________

Date: ________________

Today's Intuitions and Psychic Events: ________________________

Date: ________________

*Today's Intuitions and Psychic Events:*________________________

Date: ________________

Today's Intuitions and Psychic Events: ________________________

Date: ________________

*Today's Intuitions and Psychic Events:*________________________

Date: ________________

*Today's Intuitions and Psychic Events:*________________________

Date: ________________

Today's Intuitions and Psychic Events:

Date: ________________

Today's Intuitions and Psychic Events: ________________________

Date: ________________

*Today's Intuitions and Psychic Events:*________________________

Date: ________________

Today's Intuitions and Psychic Events: ________________________

Date: ________________

Today's Intuitions and Psychic Events: ________________________

Date: ________________

*Today's Intuitions and Psychic Events:*________________________

Date: ________________

*Today's Intuitions and Psychic Events:*________________________

Date: ________________

Today's Intuitions and Psychic Events: ______________________

Date: ________________

*Today's Intuitions and Psychic Events:*________________________

Date: ________________

*Today's Intuitions and Psychic Events:*________________________

Date: ________________

*Today's Intuitions and Psychic Events:*________________________

Date: ________________

*Today's Intuitions and Psychic Events:*________________________

Date: ________________

*Today's Intuitions and Psychic Events:*________________________

Date: ________________

Today's Intuitions and Psychic Events: ________________________

Date: ________________

*Today's Intuitions and Psychic Events:*________________________

Date: ________________

Today's Intuitions and Psychic Events: ________________________

Date: ________________

*Today's Intuitions and Psychic Events:*________________________

Date: ________________

*Today's Intuitions and Psychic Events:*________________________

Date: ________________

*Today's Intuitions and Psychic Events:*________________________

Date: ________________

Today's Intuitions and Psychic Events: ________________________

Date: ________________

*Today's Intuitions and Psychic Events:*________________________

Date: ________________

Today's Intuitions and Psychic Events: ________________________

Date: ________________

*Today's Intuitions and Psychic Events:*________________________

Date: ________________

*Today's Intuitions and Psychic Events:*________________________

Date: ________________

*Today's Intuitions and Psychic Events:*______________________

Date: ________________

Today's Intuitions and Psychic Events: ________________________

Date: ________________

*Today's Intuitions and Psychic Events:*________________________

Date: ________________

*Today's Intuitions and Psychic Events:*________________________

Date: _______________

Today's Intuitions and Psychic Events:______________________

Date: ________________

Today's Intuitions and Psychic Events: ________________________

Date: ________________

Today's Intuitions and Psychic Events:

Date: ________________

Today's Intuitions and Psychic Events: ________________________

Date: ________________

Today's Intuitions and Psychic Events: ________________________

Date: ________________

*Today's Intuitions and Psychic Events:*________________________

Date: ________________

*Today's Intuitions and Psychic Events:*________________________

Date: ________________

Today's Intuitions and Psychic Events:

Date: ________________

Today's Intuitions and Psychic Events: ________________________

Date: ________________

Today's Intuitions and Psychic Events: ________________________

Date: ________________

Today's Intuitions and Psychic Events:

Date: ________________

*Today's Intuitions and Psychic Events:*________________________

Date: ________________

*Today's Intuitions and Psychic Events:*________________________

Date: ________________

*Today's Intuitions and Psychic Events:*________________________

Date: ________________

*Today's Intuitions and Psychic Events:*________________________

Date: ________________

Today's Intuitions and Psychic Events: ________________________

Date: ________________

Today's Intuitions and Psychic Events:

Date: ________________

*Today's Intuitions and Psychic Events:*________________________

Date: ________________

*Today's Intuitions and Psychic Events:*________________________

Date: ________________

*Today's Intuitions and Psychic Events:*________________________

Date: ________________

*Today's Intuitions and Psychic Events:*________________________

Date: ________________

*Today's Intuitions and Psychic Events:*________________________

Date: ________________

Today's Intuitions and Psychic Events:

Date: ________________

Today's Intuitions and Psychic Events: ________________________

Date: ________________

*Today's Intuitions and Psychic Events:*________________________

Date: ________________

*Today's Intuitions and Psychic Events:*________________________

Date: _________________

Today's Intuitions and Psychic Events:

Date: ________________

*Today's Intuitions and Psychic Events:*________________________

Date: ______________

*Today's Intuitions and Psychic Events:*______________________

Date: ________________

*Today's Intuitions and Psychic Events:*________________________

Date: ________________

Today's Intuitions and Psychic Events: ________________________

Date: ________________

Today's Intuitions and Psychic Events: ________________________

Date: ________________

*Today's Intuitions and Psychic Events:*________________________

Date: ________________

Today's Intuitions and Psychic Events: ________________________

Date: ________________

*Today's Intuitions and Psychic Events:*________________________

Date: ________________

*Today's Intuitions and Psychic Events:*________________________

Date: ________________

*Today's Intuitions and Psychic Events:*________________________

Date: ________________

Today's Intuitions and Psychic Events: ________________________

Date: ________________

*Today's Intuitions and Psychic Events:*________________________

Date: ________________

Today's Intuitions and Psychic Events: ________________________

Date: ________________

*Today's Intuitions and Psychic Events:*________________________

Date: ________________

*Today's Intuitions and Psychic Events:*______________________

Date: ________________

*Today's Intuitions and Psychic Events:*________________________

Date: ________________

*Today's Intuitions and Psychic Events:*________________________

Date: ________________

*Today's Intuitions and Psychic Events:*________________________

Date: ________________

*Today's Intuitions and Psychic Events:*________________________

Date: ____________

Today's Intuitions and Psychic Events: ____________________

Date: ________________

Today's Intuitions and Psychic Events: ________________________

Date: ________________

*Today's Intuitions and Psychic Events:*________________________

Date: ________________

Today's Intuitions and Psychic Events: ______________________

Date: ________________

*Today's Intuitions and Psychic Events:*________________________

Date: ________________

Today's Intuitions and Psychic Events: ________________________

Date: ________________

*Today's Intuitions and Psychic Events:*________________________

Date: ________________

*Today's Intuitions and Psychic Events:*________________________

Date: ________________

Today's Intuitions and Psychic Events: ________________________

Date: ________________

*Today's Intuitions and Psychic Events:*________________________

Date: ________________

Today's Intuitions and Psychic Events:

Date: ________________

Today's Intuitions and Psychic Events:

Date: ________________

*Today's Intuitions and Psychic Events:*________________________

Date: ________________

*Today's Intuitions and Psychic Events:*________________________

Date: ________________

*Today's Intuitions and Psychic Events:*________________________

Date: ________________

Today's Intuitions and Psychic Events:

Date: ________________

*Today's Intuitions and Psychic Events:*________________________

Date: ________________

Today's Intuitions and Psychic Events: ________________________

Date: ________________

*Today's Intuitions and Psychic Events:*________________________

Date: ________________

Today's Intuitions and Psychic Events: ________________________

Date: ________________

*Today's Intuitions and Psychic Events:*____________________

Date: ________________

Today's Intuitions and Psychic Events:

Date: ________________

*Today's Intuitions and Psychic Events:*________________________

Date: ________________

*Today's Intuitions and Psychic Events:*________________________

Date: ________________

*Today's Intuitions and Psychic Events:*________________________

Date: ________________

*Today's Intuitions and Psychic Events:*________________________

Date: ________________

*Today's Intuitions and Psychic Events:*________________________

Date: ________________

*Today's Intuitions and Psychic Events:*________________________

Date: ________________

*Today's Intuitions and Psychic Events:*________________________

Date: ________________

Today's Intuitions and Psychic Events:

Date: ________________

Today's Intuitions and Psychic Events: ________________________

Date: ________________

Today's Intuitions and Psychic Events: ________________________

Date: ________________

Today's Intuitions and Psychic Events:

Date: ________________

*Today's Intuitions and Psychic Events:*________________________

Date: ________________

Today's Intuitions and Psychic Events:

Date: ________________

*Today's Intuitions and Psychic Events:*________________________

Date: ______________

Today's Intuitions and Psychic Events:

Date: ________________

Today's Intuitions and Psychic Events: ________________________

Date: ________________

*Today's Intuitions and Psychic Events:*________________________

VISIT MELISSA ALVAREZ ONLINE AT
www.MelissaA.com
www.APsychicHaven.com
Email Melissa at media@melissaa.com

www.ingramcontent.com/pod-product-compliance
Lightning Source LLC
Chambersburg PA
CBHW060156260626
47160CB00001B/287